Microsoft Excel 2016 Keyboard Shortcuts

For Macintosh

By

U. C-Abel Books.

All Rights Reserved

Table of Contents

Acknowledgement.

U. C-Abel Books will not take all credits for Microsoft Excel 2016 keyboard shortcuts listed in this book, but shares it with Microsoft Corporation because some of the shortcuts came from them and are "used with permission from Microsoft".

Dedication

This compilation is dedicated to Microsoft Excel users, Mac computer users, and lovers of keyboard shortcuts all over the world.

Introduction.

We enjoy using shortcuts because they set us on a high plane that astonishes people around us when we work with them. As wonderful shortcuts users, the worst eyesore we witness in computer operation is to see somebody sluggishly struggling to execute a task through mouse usage when in actual sense shortcuts will help to save that person time. Most people have asked us to help them with a list of keyboard shortcuts that can make them work as smartly as we do and that drove us into research to broaden our knowledge and truly help them as they demanded, that is the reason for the existence of this book. It is a great tool for lovers of shortcuts, and those who want to join the group.

Most times the things we love don't come by easily. It is our love for keyboard shortcuts that made us to bear long sleepless nights like owls just to make sure we get the best out of it, and it is the best we got that we are sharing with you in this book. You cannot be the same at computing after reading this book. The time you entrusted to our care is an expensive possession and we promise not to mess it up.

Thank you.

What to Know Before You Begin.

General Notes.

1. For effective use of keyboard shortcuts listed in this book, JAWS users must turn off Virtual Ribbon Menu feature.

2. Most of the keyboard shortcuts you will see in this book refer to the U.S. keyboard layout. Keys for other layouts might not correspond exactly to the keys on a U.S. keyboard. Keyboard shortcuts for laptop computers might also differ.

3. It is important to note that when using shortcuts to perform any command, you should make sure the target area is active, if not you may get a wrong result. Example, if you want to highlight all texts you must make sure the text field is active and if an object, make sure the object area is active. The active area is always known by the location where the cursor of your computer blinks.

4. On a Mac keyboard, the Command key is denoted with the ⌘symbol.

5. The settings in some versions of the Macintosh operating system and some utility applications might conflict with keyboard shortcuts and function key operations in Office.

6. If a function key doesn't work as you expect it to, press the Fn key in addition to the function key. If you don't want to press the Fn key every time, you can change your Apple system preferences.

7. The plus (+) sign that comes in the middle of keyboard shortcuts simply means the keys are meant to be combined or held down together not to be added as one of the shortcut keys. In a case where plus sign is needed; it will be duplicated (++).
8. Many keyboards assign special functions to function keys, by default. To use the function key for other purposes, you have to press Fn+the function key.
9. For keyboard shortcuts in which you press one key immediately followed by another key, the keys are separated by a comma (,).

10. It is also important to note that the keyboard shortcuts listed in this book are for Microsoft Excel 2016 for Mac.

Other Areas to Take Note of.

Common Office For Mac Keyboard Shortcuts

The common office for mac keyboard shortcuts listed in this book are applicable to Excel 2016 for Mac, PowerPoint 2016 for Mac, Word for Mac 2016, Outlook 2016 for Mac, Word for Mac 2011, Excel for Mac 2011, Outlook for Mac 2011, and PowerPoint for Mac 2011.

Create a custom keyboard shortcut for Office 2016 for Mac.

The steps written on how to create a custom keyboard shortcuts for office 2016 for mac applies to all Office for Mac programs.

Excel for Mac

Excel keyboard shortcuts listed in this section are for use in Excel 2016 for Mac. If you use Excel on a Windows computer, many of the shortcuts that use the CTRL key also work in Excel 2016 for Mac. However, not all do. When in doubt, consult this list.

Some Short Forms You Will Find in This Book and Their Full Meaning.

Here are short forms used in this Microsoft Excel 2016 Keyboard Shortcuts For Macintosh book and their full meaning.

1.	Win	-	Windows logo key
2.	Tab	-	Tabulate Key
3.	Shft	-	Shift Key
4.	Prt sc	-	Print Screen
5.	Num Lock	-	Number Lock Key
6.	F	-	Function Key
7.	Esc	-	Escape Key
8.	Ctrl	-	Control Key
9.	Caps Lock	-	Caps Lock Key
10.	Alt	-	Alternate Key

CHAPTER 1.

About Office 2016 and Mac.

Introduction to Microsoft Office.

Microsoft Office is a computer software that is made up of apps, servers and services, developed and marketed by Microsoft Corporation.

Definition of Macintosh.

Macintosh is a popular model of computer manufactured and marketed by Apple Inc. that features a graphical user interface which uses windows, icons, and a mouse to make it relatively easy for newbies/novices to use the computer effectively.

Differences between (Macintosh) Macs and Personal Computers (Pcs). By www.diffen.com

A **PC** generally refers to a computer that runs on the Windows operating system. It is also defined as an IBM-compatible computer, thereby meaning that its architecture is based on the IBM microprocessor. A number of different operating systems are compatible with PCs; the most popular of which is Microsoft Windows. Some others are the UNIX variants, such as Linux, FreeBSD, and Solaris.

On the other hand **Macintosh**, commonly known as **Mac**, is a brand name which covers several lines of personal computers designed, developed, and marketed by Apple Inc. The Mac is the only computer in the world that can run all the major operating systems, including Mac OS X, Windows XP, and Vista. With software like Parallels Desktop or VMware Fusion they can be run; side by side.

Macs and PCs both have dedicated followers, and each type of computer has its own strengths and weaknesses.

Mac		PC
What is it?	Short form for "Macintosh" and refers to any computer produced by Apple, Inc.	Refers to any computer running IBM-Based (Windows, Linux, Solaris, FreeBSD) operating systems. stands for "Personal Computer"
Cost	Computers start at $499 for the Mac Mini desktop, $899 for the Macbook Air notebook, and	Compared to a Mac, Windows and Windows-associated hardware is

	$1099 for the iMac all-in-one. Other models are more expensive. For desktop or home use Macs are generally expensive than a PC.	cheaper, and you can build your own for even less money. Comparable computers running Windows can be found around 40% cheaper than a Mac.
Manufacturer	Apple Inc	Several companies: HP, Toshiba, Dell, Lenovo, Samsung, Acer, Gateway etc.
Development and Distribution	Macs are developed and distributed by Apple Inc.	PCs are manufactured and distributed by hundreds of manufacturers.
Company / developer	Apple, Inc.	Microsoft (Windows), Ubuntu (Linux), Sun (Solaris), etc.
Gaming	Not as many games are made natively for the Mac, although in recent years, many more applications are released for them. The App Store is a hub for users to	The library of games available for the PC is exhaustive, and hardware specifically tweaked for gaming

	download games from.	performance is much more readily available for Windows. The array of graphics cards and upgradability also favor Windows-based computers.
User	Home users and businesses (mainly in the creative department)	Home users and businesses
Available language(s)	Multilingual	Must purchase a different OS Version, but has multiple languages available.
OS family	Unix-like (BSD>Darwin>Mac)	Windows, Linux, Solaris, FreeBSD, etc.
Popular Applications	Photos, iMovie, GarageBand, Pages, Numbers, Keynote, Safari, Mail, Messages, FaceTime, Calendar, Contacts, App Store, iTunes, iBooks, Maps, Photo Booth, Time Machine	MS Office, Internet Explorer, Media Player, Media Center, Windows Defender, SkyDrive, VLC media player, Chrome browser

Latest Operating System	OS X Yosemite (version 10.10); OS X El Capitan (version 10.11) announced	Windows 8/8.1, Windows 10 announced
Compatibility	Can open almost all PC files and can coexist on local networks with PCs. Can open .doc, .exe (as a compressed bundle), .xls, and others. Software exists for other file types. Can also run Windows on a Mac for 100% compatibility.	Mac-based files (.DMG) cannot be opened on PCs natively, but you can install software that can read, and possibly write Mac-based files on a PC.
Supported architectures	Intel Microprocessors	Intel and AMD processors
Market Reach	Attracts graphic designers, video and music producers, tech journalists, app developers etc.	Wide reach to all stratas. Business users tend to use Windows hardware due to compatibility.
Virus Attacks	Since Macs are not as popular as PCs, there are fewer malware written to target Macs, although the threat of malicious software is growing, like from Java.	Being the popular desktop choice, most virus writers target Windows systems, however, Linux often has less malware.

Compatible Operating Systems	OS X, Windows (through virtual machine or Boot Camp), Linux	Windows, Linux
Performance	Since Apple have controlled the hardware & software bundles and model updates, so every Mac operates smoothly without worry on lagging, incompatibles, and have stable and expected performance	Different OEMs and even custom build PCs might not have the suitable drivers released for every components in each OS version, incompatibles, lagging may occur. Maybe cannot reach expected performance
Repairs	Any knowledgeable person can perform repairs and upgrades. Local computer-help stores can also be contacted for repairs. AppleCare can extend the warranty. Newer Macs are becoming less upgrade-friendly, though.	Any knowledgeable person can perform repairs and upgrades. Local computer-help stores can also be contacted for repairs. OEMs and component shops provides limited warranty.

Programs and apps	Same as gaming, limited choice due to user range.	Same as gaming, excess choice due to user range.
Piracy Prevention	Activation is not required, can reinstall as many times as needed.	Windows has a unique activation key for each package distribution, and lots of custom and OEM PC appears, so genuine checking become important. Linux, Solaris, FreeBSD is free and no need for those keys.
Customizability	No	Yes
Messaging	Messages (using iMessage, Google Talk, etc.)	Skype, Facebook, and Twitter
Voice commands	Yes	Yes
Maps	Yes	Yes
Internet browsing	Safari, Chrome, Firefox, plus many more.	Internet Explorer, Chrome, Firefox, Safari (no longer supported)
App store	App Store	Windows Store
Widgets	Yes	Yes

Working state	Current	Current
Interface	Mouse, keyboard, trackpad, other peripherals	Mouse, keyboard, trackpad, other peripherals
Has Registry	No	Yes
Overclockable	No	Yes, depends on CPU and Motherboard

Introduction to Office 2016 for Mac.

Office 2016 is an office suite developed and sold by Microsoft. The preview version of Microsoft Office for Mac was released on 5th March 2015, then the final version was released on 5th July 2015 by Microsoft Corporation.

Supported languages in Office 2016 for Mac

Office 2016 for Mac is currently available in the following languages:

- Arabic
- Brazilian Portuguese
- Chinese (Simplified)
- Chinese (Traditional)
- Czech
- Danish
- Dutch
- English

- Finnish
- French
- Hebrew
- German
- Italian
- Japanese
- Norwegian Bokmal
- Polish
- Russian
- Spanish
- Swedish
- Thai

The Difference between Office 365 and Office 2016.

Office 365 is a subscription service (this means you pay for it on monthly or yearly basis) provided by Microsoft Corporation that includes the most recent version of office, which currently is also called office 2016. Some of the office 365 plans like HOME, let you share your subscription with people around you.

Contrariwise, Office 2016 is marketed as a one-time purchase bundle, this simply means you pay a single upfront cost to receive Office programs/applications for your personal or Macintosh computer. No upgrade option.

The major difference is that Office 365 has an upgrade option while office 2016 doesn't, this means that after you have purchased Office 2016 bundle, you will have to purchase another in future if there is an upgrade (added feature) you desire.

CHAPTER 2.

Fundamental Knowledge of Keyboard Shortcuts.

Without the existence of keyboard, there wouldn't have been anything like keyboard shortcuts so in this chapter we will learn a little about the computer keyboard before moving to keyboard shortcuts.

1. Definition of Computer Keyboard.

This is an input device that is used to send data to computer memory.

Sketch of a Keyboard

1.1 Types of Keyboard.

i. Standard (Basic) Keyboard.
ii. Enhanced (Extended) Keyboard.

i. **Standard Keyboard:** This is a keyboard designed during the 1800s for mechanical typewriters with just 10 function keys (F keys) placed at the left side of it.

ii. **Enhanced Keyboard:** This is the current 101 to 102-key keyboard that is included in almost all the personal computers (PCs) of nowadays, which has 12 function keys at the top side of it.

Function Keys

Numeric Keys

Alphabetic keys

1.2 Segments of the keyboard

- Numeric keys
- Alphabetic keys
- Punctuation keys
- Windows Logo key.
- Function keys
- Special keys

Numeric Keys: Numeric keys are keys with numbers from **0 - 9**.

Alphabetic Keys: These are keys that have alphabets on them, ranging from **A** to **Z**.

Punctuation Keys: These are keys of the keyboard used for punctuation, examples include comma, full stop, colon, question marks, hyphen, etc.

Windows Logo Key: A key on Microsoft Computer keyboard with its logo displayed on it. Search for this on your keyboard.

Apple Key: This also known as Command key is a modifier key that you can find on an Apple keyboard. It usually has the image of an apple or command logo on it. Search for this on your Apple keyboard

Function Keys: These are keys that have **F** on them which are usually combined with other keys. They are F1 - F12, and are also in the class called *Special Keys*.

Special Keys: These are keys that perform special functions. They include: Tab, Ctrl, Caps lock, Insert, Prt sc, alt gr, Shift, Home, Num lock, Esc and many others. Special keys differs according to the type of computer involved. In some keyboard layout, especially laptops, the keys that turn the speaker on/off, the one that increases/decreases volume, the key that turns the computer Wifi on/off are also special keys.

Other Special Keys Worthy of Note.

Enter Key: This is located at the right-hand corner of most keyboards. It is used to send messages to the computer to execute commands, in most cases it is used to mean "Ok" or "Go".

Escape Key (ESC): This is the first key on the upper left of most keyboards. It is used to cancel routines, close menus and select options such as **Save** according to circumstance.

Control Key (CTRL): It is located on the bottom row of the left and right hand side of the keyboard. They also work with the function keys to execute commands using Keyboard shortcuts (key combinations).

Alternate Key (ALT): It is located on the bottom row also of some keyboard, very close to the CTRL key on both side of the keyboard. It enables many editing functions to be accomplished by using some keystroke combinations on the keyboard.

Shift Key: This adds to the roles of function keys. In addition, it enables the use of alternative function of a particular button (key), especially, those with more than one function on a key. E.g. use of capital letters, symbols and numbers.

1.3. Selecting/Highlighting With Keyboard.

This is a highlighting method or style where data is selected using keyboard instead of a computer mouse.

To do this:

- Move your cursor to the text you want to highlight, make sure that area is active
- Hold down the shift key with one finger
- Then use another finger to move the arrow key that points to the direction you want to highlight.

1.4 The Operating Modes Of The Keyboard.

Just like mouse, keyboard has two operating modes. The two modes are Text Entering Mode and Command Mode.

a. **Text Entering Mode:** this mode gives the operator/user the opportunity to type text.
b. **Command Mode:** this is used to command the operating system/software/application to execute commands in certain ways.

2. Ways To Improve In Your Typing Skill.

1. Put Your Eyes Off The Keyboard.

This is the aspect of keyboard usage that many don't find funny because they always ask. "How can I put my eyes off the keyboard when I am running away from the occurrence of errors on my file?" My aim is to be fast, is this not going to slow me down?

Of course, there will be errors and at the same time your speed will slow down but the motive behind the introduction to this method is to make you faster than you are. Looking at your keyboard while you type can make you get a sore neck, it is better you learn to touch type because the more you type with your eyes fixed on the screen instead of the keyboard, the faster you become.

An alternative to keeping your eyes off your keyboard is to use the *"Das Keyboard Ultimate"*.

2. Errors Challenge You
It is better to fail than not trying at all. Not trying at all is an attribute of the weak and lazybones. When you make mistakes, try again because errors are opportunities for improvement.

3. Good Posture (Position Yourself Well).
Do not adopt an awkward position while typing. You should get everything on your desk organized or arranged before sitting to type. Your posture while typing contributes to your speed and productivity.

4. Practice

Here is the conclusion of everything said above. You have to practice your shortcuts constantly. The practice alone is a way of improvement. "Practice brings improvement". Practice always.

2.1 Software That Will Help You Improve Your Typing Skill.

There are several Software programs for typing that both kids and adults can use for their typing skill. Here is a list of software that can help you improve in your typing: Mavis Beacon, Typing Instructor, Mucky Typing Adventure, Rapid Tying Tutor, Letter Chase Tying Tutor, Alice Touch Typing Tutor and many more. Personally, I recommend Mavis Beacon.

To learn typing with MAVIS BEACON, install Mavis Beacon software to your computer, start with keyboard lesson, then move to games. Games like *Penguin Crossing, Creature Lab* or *Space Junk* will help you become a professional in typing. Typing and keyboard shortcuts work hand-in-hand.

Sketch of a computer mouse

Right Mouse button

Scroll button

Left Mouse button

3. Mouse:

This is an oval-shaped portable input device with three buttons for scrolling, left clicking, and right clicking that enables work to be done effectively on a computer. The plural form of mouse is mice.

3.1 Types of Computer Mouse

- Mechanical Mouse
- Optical Mechanical Mouse (Optomechanical)
- Laser Mouse
- Optical Mouse
- BlueTrack Mouse

3.2 Forms of Clicking:

Left Clicking: This is the process of clicking the left side button of the mouse. It can also be called *clicking* without the addition of *left*.

Right Clicking: It is the process of clicking the right side button of a computer mouse.

Double Clicking: It is the process of clicking the left side button two times (twice) and immediately.

Double clicking is used to select a word while thrice clicking is used to select a sentence or paragraph.

Scroll Button: It is the little key attached to the mouse that looks like a tiny wheel. It takes you up and down a page when moved.

3.3 Mouse Pad: This is a small soft mat that is placed under the mouse to make it have a free movement.

3.4 Laptop Mouse Touchpad

This unlike the mouse we explained above is not external, rather it is inbuilt (comes with a laptop computer). With the presence of a laptop mouse touchpad, an external mouse is not needed to use a laptop, except in a case where it is malfunctioning or the operator prefers to use external one for some reasons.

The laptop mouse touchpad is usually positioned at the end of the keyboard section of a laptop computer. It is rectangular in shape with two buttons positioned below it. The two buttons/keys are used for left and right clicking just like the external mouse. Some laptops come with four mouse keys. Two placed above the mouse for left and right clicking and two other keys placed below it for the same function.

4. Definition Of Keyboard Shortcuts.

Keyboard shortcuts are defined as a series of keys, sometimes with combination that execute tasks that typically involve the use of mouse or other input devices.

5. Why You Should Use Shortcuts.

1. One may not be able to use a computer mouse easily because of disability or pain.

2. One may not be able to see the mouse pointer as a result of vision impairment, in such case what will the person do? The answer is SHORTCUT.

3. Research has made it known that Extensive mouse usage is related to Repetitive Syndrome Injury (RSI) greatly than the use of keyboard.

4. Keyboard shortcuts speed up computer users, making learning them a worthwhile effort.

5. When performing a job that requires precision, it is wise that you use the keyboard instead of mouse, for instance, if you are dealing with Text Editing, it is better you handle it using keyboard shortcuts than spending more time with your computer mouse alone.

6. Studies calculate that using keyboard shortcuts allows working 10 times faster than working with the mouse. The time you spend looking for the mouse and then getting the cursor to the position you want is lost! Reducing your work duration by 10 times brings you greater results.

5.1 Ways To Become A Lover Of Shortcuts.

1. Always have the urge to learn new shortcut keys associated with the programs you use.
2. Be happy whenever you learn a new shortcut.

3. Try as much as you can to apply the new shortcuts you learnt.

4. Always bear it in mind that learning new shortcuts is worth it.

5. Always remember that the use of keyboard shortcuts keeps people healthy while performing computer activities.

5.2 How To Learn New Shortcut Keys

1. Do a research for them: quick reference (a cheat sheet comprehensively compiled like ours) can go a long way to help you improve.

2. Buy applications that show you keyboard shortcuts every time you execute an action with mouse.

3. Disconnect your mouse if you must learn this fast.

4. Read user manuals and help topics (Whether offline or online).

5.3 Your Reward For Knowing Shortcut Keys.

1. You will get faster unimaginably.

2. Your level of efficiency will increase.

3. You will find it easy to use.

4. Opportunities are high that you will become an expert in what you do.

5. You won't have to go for **Office button**, click **New,** click **Blank and Recent** and click **Create** just to insert a fresh/blank page. **Ctrl +N** takes care of that in a second.

A Funny Note: Keyboarding and Mousing are in a marital union with Keyboarding being the head, so it will be unfair for anybody to put asunder between them.

5.4 Why We Emphasize On The Use of Shortcuts.

You may never ditch your mouse completely unless you are ready to make your brain a box of keyboard shortcuts which will really be frustrating, just imagine yourself learning all shortcuts that go with the programs you use and their various versions. You shouldn't learn keyboard shortcuts that way.

Why we are emphasizing on the use of shortcuts is because mouse usage is becoming unusually common and unhealthy, too. So we just want to make sure both are combined so you can get fast, productive and healthy in your computer activities. All you need to know is just the most important ones associated with the programs you use.

CHAPTER 3.

How to Download, Install, Launch, and Uninstall Office 2016 for Mac.

Download and Install Office 2016 for Mac

1. Go to your **My Account** page at Office.com and sign in with your Microsoft account.
2. On the **My Account** page, under the name of your subscription, select **Install**.

3. On the next page, under **Install information**, select **Install** to begin downloading the installation package.

4. Once the download has completed, open Finder, go to **Downloads**, and double-click **Microsoft_Office_2016_Installer.pkg** (the name might vary slightly).

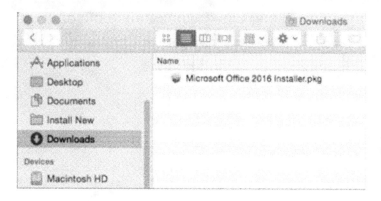

Tip: If you see an error that the Microsoft_Office_2016_Installer.pkg can't be opened because it is from an unidentified developer, wait 10 seconds and then try double-clicking the installer package again. If you are stuck at the **Verifying....** progress bar, close or cancel the progress bar and try again.

5. On the first installation screen, select **Continue** to begin the installation process.

6. Review the software license agreement, and then click **Continue**.

7. Select **Agree** to agree to the terms of the software license agreement.

8. Review the disk space requirements, and then click **Install**.

9. Enter your Mac login password, if prompted, and then click **Install Software**. (This is the password that you use to log in to your Mac.)

10. The software begins to install. Click **Close** when the installation is finished.

Launch an Office for Mac app and start the activation process.

1. Click the **Launchpad** icon in the Dock to display all of your apps.

2. Click the **Microsoft Word** icon in the Launchpad.

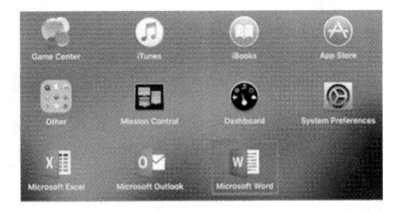

3. The **What's New** window opens automatically when you launch Word. Click **Get Started** to start activating.

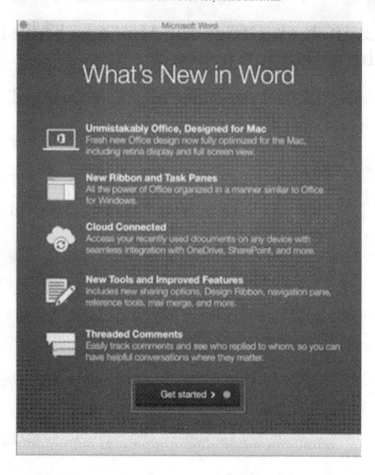

Installation notes

Can I install Office 2016 for Mac and Office for Mac 2011 on the same computer?

Yes, you can install and use Office 2016 for Mac and Office for Mac 2011 at the same time just like Office 2016 and Office 2013 for Windows. However, we recommend that you uninstall Office for Mac 2011 before you install the new version just to prevent any confusion.

How do I pin the Office app icons to the dock?

1. Go to **Finder** > **Applications** and open the Office app you want.
2. In the Dock, Control+click or right-click the app icon and choose **Options** > **Keep in Dock**.

Uninstall Office 2016 for Mac.

Applies To: Excel 2016 for Mac, Outlook 2016 for Mac, PowerPoint 2016 for Mac, Word 2016 for Mac, and OneNote 2016 for Mac.

To uninstall Office 2016 for Mac, move the applications and user preference files to the Trash. Once you've removed everything, empty the Trash and restart your Mac to complete the process.

You must be signed in as an administrator or provide an administrator name and password to complete these steps.

Remove Office 2016 for Mac Applications.

1. Open Finder and click **Applications**.
2. Command ⌘+click to select all of the Office 2016 for Mac applications.
3. Ctrl+click or right-click the applications you selected and click **Move to Trash**.

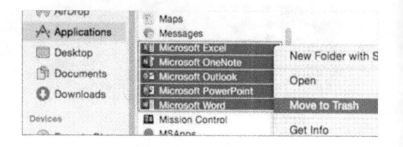

Remove Files from Your User Library Folder.

To remove files from your user **Library** folder, you'll need to first set the Finder View options.

1. In Finder, press ⌘+**Shift+h**.
2. On the Finder menu, click **View** > **as List**, and then click **View** > **Show View Options**.

3. In the **View Options** dialog box, select **Show Library Folder**.

4. Switch back to Column view (⌘+3) and click **<YourUserName>Library** > **Containers** and ctrl+click or right-click each of these folders if present, and then click **Move to Trash**.
   - ○ **com.microsoft.errorreporting**
   - ○ **com.microsoft.Excel**
   - ○ **com.microsoft.netlib.shipassertproc ess**
   - ○ **com.microsoft.Office365ServiceV2**
   - ○ **com.microsoft.Outlook**
   - ○ **com.microsoft.Powerpoint**
   - ○ **com.microsoft.RMS-XPCService**
   - ○ **com.microsoft.Word**
   - ○ **com.microsoft.onenote.mac**

5. **Warning:** Outlook data will be removed when you move the three folders listed in this step to **Trash**. You should back up these folders before you delete them.

Switch back to Column view (⌘+3) and click **<YourUserName>Library** > **Group**

Containers and ctrl+click or right-click each of these folders if present, and then click **Move to Trash.**

- ○ **UBF8T346G9.ms**
- ○ **UBF8T346G9.Office**
- ○ **UBF8T346G9.OfficeOsfWebHost**

CHAPTER 4.

15 (Fifteen) Special Keyboard Shortcuts.

The fifteen special keyboard shortcuts are fifteen (15) shortcuts every computer user should know.

The following is a list of keyboard shortcuts every computer user should know.

1. **Ctrl + A:** Control plus A, highlights or selects everything you have in the environment where you are working.

   *If you are like **"Wow, the content of this document is large and there is no time to select all of it, besides, it's going to mount pressure on my computer?"** Using the mouse for this is an outdated method of handling a task like selecting all, Ctrl+A will take care of that in a second.*

2. **Ctrl + C:** Control plus C copies any highlighted or selected element within the work environment.

   Saves the time and stress which would have been used to right click and click again just to copy. Use ctrl+c.

3. **Ctrl + N:** Control plus N opens a new window. *Instead of clicking* **File, New, blank/ template** *and another* **click,** *just press Ctrl + N and a fresh window will appear instantly.*

4. **Ctrl + O:** Control plus O opens a new program. *Use ctrl +O when you want to locate / open a file or program.*

5. **Ctrl + P:** Control plus P prints the active document. *Always use this to locate the printer dialog box, and thereafter print.*

6. **Ctrl + S:** Control plus S saves a new document or file and changes made by the user. *Please stop! Don't use the mouse. Just press Ctrl+S and everything will be saved.*

7. **Ctrl +V:** Control plus V pastes copied elements into the active area of the program in use. *Using ctrl+V in a case like this Saves the time and stress of right clicking and clicking again just to paste.*

8. **Ctrl + W:** Control plus W is used to close the page you are working on when you want to leave the work environment.

"There is a way Debby does this without using the mouse. Oh my God, why didn't I learn it then?" Don't worry, I have the answer. Debby presses Ctrl+W to close active windows.

9. **Ctrl + X:** Control plus X cuts elements (making the elements to disappear from their original place). The difference between cutting and deleting elements is that in Cutting, what was cut doesn't get lost permanently but prepares itself so that it can be pasted on another location selected by the user.

    *Use ctrl+x when you think **"this shouldn't be here and I can't stand the stress of retyping or redesigning it in the rightful place it belongs".***

10. **Ctrl + Y:** Control plus Y redoes an undone action.

    Ctrl+Z brought back what you didn't need? Press Ctrl+ Y to remove it again.

11. **Ctrl + Z:** Control plus Z undoes actions.
    Can't find what you typed now or a picture you inserted, it suddenly disappeared or you mistakenly removed it? Press Ctrl+Z to bring it back.

12. **Alt + F4:** Alternative plus F4 closes active windows or items.

*You don't need to move the mouse in order to close an active window, just press **Alt** + **F4** if you are done or don't want somebody who is coming to see what you are doing.*

13. **Ctrl + F6:** Control plus F6 Navigates between open windows, making it possible for a user to see what is happening in windows that are active.

    Are you working in Microsoft Word and want to find out if the other active window where your browser is loading a page is still progressing? Use Ctrl + F6.

14. **F1:** This displays the help window.

    *Is your computer malfunctioning? Use **F1** to find help when you don't know what next to do.*

15. **F12:** This enables user to make changes to an already saved document.

    F12 is the shortcut to use when you want to change the format in which you saved your existing document, password it, change its name, change the file location or destination, or make other changes to it. It will save your time.

CHAPTER 5.

Common Office for Mac Keyboard Shortcuts.

Here are common shortcuts you can use when working with your Mac computer.

Working With Files, Applications, And Tools

TASK	SHORTCUT
Create a new file or Outlook item	Command + N
Create a new file from a template or theme	SHIFT + Command + P
Expand or minimize the ribbon	Command + OPTION + R
Save	Command + S
Print	Command + P
Open a file	Command + O
Close a file	Command + W
Quit the current application	Command + Q
Hide the current application	Command + H
Hide other applications	OPTION + Command + H
Minimize the window	Command + M

Editing And Formatting

TASK	SHORTCUT
Undo the last change	Command + Z
Redo or repeat the last action	Command + Y
Cut the selection (and copy to clipboard)	Command + X
Copy the selection to the clipboard	Command + C
Copy the formatting from the selection	Command + SHIFT + C
Copy the selection to Scrapbook	CONTROL + OPTION + C
Paste	Command + V
Paste Special	Command + CONTROL + V
Paste the formatting to the selection	Command + SHIFT + V
Select All	Command + A
Find	Command + F
Insert hyperlink	Command + K

Dialog Boxes

TASK	SHORTCUT
Move to the next text box in a dialog box	TAB
Move to the previous box, option, control, or command in a dialog box	SHIFT + TAB
Exit a dialog box or cancel an action	ESC

Create A Custom Keyboard Shortcut For Office 2016 For Mac.

To create custom keyboard shortcuts in Office for Mac, use the built-in capability in Mac OS X.

1. From the **Apple** menu, click **System Preferences** > **Keyboard** > **Shortcuts** > **App Shortcuts**.
2. Click the + sign to add a keyboard shortcut.

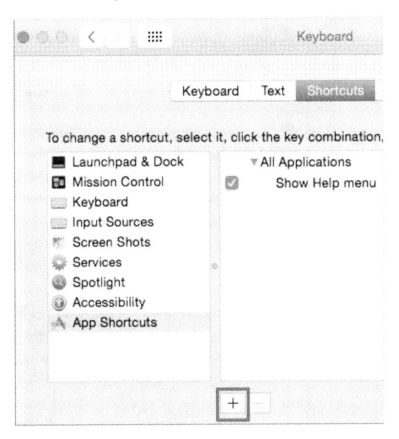

3. In the **Application** menu, click the Office for Mac app (**Microsoft Excel**, **Microsoft Word**, **Microsoft PowerPoint**, **Microsoft OneNote**, **Microsoft Outlook**) you want to create keyboard a shortcut for.

4. Enter a **Menu Title** and the **Keyboard Shortcut** and click **Add**.

Tip: If you aren't sure what the menu name is for a command, click **Help** in that app and search for what you want, which will then show you the exact menu name.

CHAPTER 6.

Keyboard Shortcuts In Excel 2016 for Mac.

Definition of Program: Microsoft Excel for Mac is an electronic spreadsheet program developed and sold by Microsoft Corporation that enables its users to create, organize, format, and calculate data. It was first released for Macintosh in the year 1985 and later on released for Windows in 1987.

The following list contains keyboard shortcuts that will boost your productivity in Microsoft Excel 2016 for Mac.

Frequently Used Shortcuts

TASK	SHORTCUT
Paste	⌘ + V or CONTROL + V
Copy	⌘ + C or CONTROL + C
Clear	DELETE

Save	⌘+ S or CONTROL + S
Undo	⌘+ Z or CONTROL + Z
Redo	⌘+ SHIFT+ Z
Cut	⌘+ X or CONTROL + X
Bold	⌘+ B or CONTROL + B
Print	⌘+ P or CONTROL + P
Open Visual Basic	OPTION + F11
Fill Down	⌘+ D or CONTROL + D
Fill Right	⌘+ R or CONTROL + R
Insert cells	CONTROL + SHIFT + =
Delete cells	⌘+ HYPHEN or CONTROL + HYPHEN
Calculate all open workbooks	⌘+ = or F9

Close window	⌘+ W or CONTROL + W
Quit Excel	⌘+ Q
Display the **Go To** dialog box	CONTROL + G or F5
Display the **Format Cells** dialog box	⌘+ 1 or CONTROL + 1
Display the **Replace** dialog box	CONTROL + H or ⌘+ SHIFT + H
Paste Special	⌘+ OPTION + V
Underline	⌘+ U
Italic	⌘+ I or CONTROL + I
New blank workbook	⌘+ N or CONTROL + N
New workbook from template	⌘+ SHIFT + P
Display the **Save As** dialog box	⌘+ SHIFT + S or F12
Display the **Help** window	F1 or ⌘+ /
Select All	⌘+ SHIFT + SPACEBAR
Add or remove a filter	⌘+ SHIFT + F or

	CONTROL + SHIFT + L
Minimize or maximize the ribbon tabs	⌘+ OPTION + R
Display the **Open** dialog box	⌘+ O or CONTROL + O
Check spelling	F7
Open the thesaurus	SHIFT + F7
Display the **Formula Builder**	SHIFT + F3
Open the **Define Name** dialog box	⌘+ F3
Open the **Create names** dialog box	⌘+ SHIFT + F3
Insert a new sheet. **	SHIFT + F11

** This shortcut conflicts with a default Mac OS key assignment. To use this shortcut, you must change your Mac keyboard settings. Go to **Apple** > **System Preferences** > **Keyboard** > **Shortcuts**. Click **Mission Control**, and then click to deselect the **Show Desktop** option.

Function Keys

Note: If a function key doesn't work as you expect it to, press the **FN** key in addition to the function key. If you don't want to press the FN key each time, you can change your system preferences: Go to **Apple** > **System Preferences** > **Keyboard**. Then select the check box for **Use all F1, F2, etc. as standard function keys.**

TASK	SHORTCUT
Display the **Help** window	F1
Edit the selected cell	F2
Insert or edit a cell comment	SHIFT + F2
Open the **Save** dialog box	OPTION + F2
Open the Formula Builder	SHIFT + F3
Open the **Define Name** dialog box	⌘+ F3
Close	⌘+ F4
Display the **Go To** dialog box	F5
Display the **Find** dialog box	SHIFT + F5
Move to the **Search Sheet** box	CONTROL + F5
Check spelling	F7
Open thesaurus	SHIFT + F7
Extend the selection	F8
Add to the selection	SHIFT + F8
Display the **Macro** dialog box	OPTION + F8
Calculate all open workbooks.	F9
Calculate the active sheet	SHIFT + F9
Minimize the active window	CONTROL + F9
Display a contextual menu, or "right click" menu	SHIFT + F10
Maximize or restore the active window	CONTROL + F10 or ⌘+ F10
Insert a new chart sheet. **	F11
Insert a new sheet **	SHIFT + F11

Insert an Excel 4.0 macro sheet	⌘+ F11
Open Visual Basic	OPTION + F11
Display the **Save As** dialog box	F12
Display the **Open** dialog box	⌘+ F12

** This shortcut conflicts with a default Mac OS key assignment. To use this shortcut, you must change your Mac keyboard settings. Go to **Apple> System Preferences> Keyboard> Shortcuts**. Click **Mission Control**, and then click to deselect the **Show Desktop** option.

Move and Scroll in a Sheet or Workbook

TASK	SHORTCUT
Move one cell up, down, left, or right	An arrow key
Move to the edge of the current data region	⌘+ arrow key
Move to the beginning of the row	HOME
Move to the beginning of the sheet	CONTROL + HOME
Move to the last cell in use on the sheet	CONTROL + END
Move down one screen	PAGE DOWN On a MacBook, press FN + DOWN ARROW
Move up one screen	PAGE UP On a MacBook, press FN + UP ARROW

Move one screen to the right	OPTION + PAGE DOWN
Move one screen to the left	OPTION + PAGE UP
Move to the next sheet in the workbook	CONTROL + PAGE DOWN or OPTION + RIGHT ARROW
Move to the previous sheet in the workbook	CONTROL + PAGE DOWN or OPTION + LEFT ARROW
Scroll to display the active cell	CONTROL + DELETE
Display the **Go To** dialog box	CONTROL + G
Display the **Find** dialog box	CONTROL + F or SHIFT + F5
Access the **Search Sheet** box	⌘ + F
Move between unlocked cells on a protected sheet	TAB

Print

TASK	SHORTCUT
Print	⌘ + P or CONTROL + P

Print preview	⌘+ P or CONTROL + P

Enter Data on a Sheet

Note: If a function key doesn't work as you expect it to, press the **FN** key in addition to the function key. If you don't want to press the FN key each time, you can change your system preferences: Go to **Apple** > **System Preferences** > **Keyboard**. Then select the check box for **Use all F1, F2, etc. as standard function keys**.

TASK	SHORTCUT
Edit the selected cell	F2
Complete a cell entry and move forward in the selection	RETURN
Start a new line in the same cell	CONTROL + OPTION + RETURN
Fill the selected cell range with the text that you type	⌘+ RETURN or CONTROL + RETURN
Complete a cell entry and move up in the selection	SHIFT + RETURN
Complete a cell entry and move to the right in the selection	TAB

Complete a cell entry and move to the left in the selection	SHIFT + TAB
Cancel a cell entry	ESC
Delete the character to the left of the insertion point, or delete the selection	DELETE
Delete the character to the right of the insertion point, or delete the selection Note: Some smaller keyboards do not have this key	⌦
Delete text to the end of the line Note: Some smaller keyboards do not have this key	CONTROL + ⌦
Move one character up, down, left, or right	An arrow key
Move to the beginning of the line	HOME
Insert a comment	SHIFT + F2
Open and edit a cell comment	SHIFT + F2
Fill down	CONTROL + D or ⌘ + D
Fill to the right	CONTROL + R or ⌘ + R
Define a name	CONTROL + L

Work in Cells or the Formula Bar

Note: If a function key doesn't work as you expect it to, press the **FN** key in addition to the function key. If you don't want to press the FN key each time, you can change your system preferences: Go to **Apple** > **System Preferences** > **Keyboard**. Then select the check box for **Use all F1, F2, etc. as standard function keys**.

TASK	SHORTCUT
Edit the selected cell	F2
Edit the active cell and then clear it, or delete the preceding character in the active cell as you edit the cell contents	DELETE
Complete a cell entry	RETURN
Enter a formula as an array formula	⌘+ SHIFT + RETURN or CONTROL + SHIFT + RETURN
Cancel an entry in the cell or formula bar	ESC
Display the Formula Builder after you type a valid function name in a formula	CONTROL + A
Insert a hyperlink	⌘+ K or CONTROL + K
Edit the active cell and position the insertion point at the end of the line	CONTROL + U
Open the Formula Builder	SHIFT + F3

Calculate the active sheet	SHIFT + F9
Display a contextual menu	SHIFT + F10
Start a formula	=
Toggle the formula reference style between absolute, relative, and mixed	⌘+ T or F4
Insert the AutoSum formula	⌘+ SHIFT + T
Enter the date	CONTROL + SEMICOLON (;)
Enter the time	⌘+ SEMICOLON (;)
Copy the value from the cell above the active cell into the cell or the formula bar	CONTROL + SHIFT + INCH MARK (")
Alternate between displaying cell values and displaying cell formulas	CONTROL + GRAVE ACCENT (`)
Copy a formula from the cell above the active cell into the cell or the formula bar	CONTROL + APOSTROPHE (')
Display the AutoComplete list	CONTROL + OPTION + DOWN ARROW
Define a name	CONTROL + L
Open the **Smart Lookup** pane	CONTROL + OPTION + ⌘+ L

Format and Edit Data

TASK	SHORTCUT
Edit the selected cell	F2

Create a table	⌘+ T or CONTROL + T
Insert a line break in a cell	⌘+ OPTION + RETURN or CONTROL + OPTION + RETURN
Insert special characters like symbols, including Emoji	CONTROL + ⌘+ SPACEBAR
Increase font size	⌘+ SHIFT + >
Decrease font size	⌘+ SHIFT + <
Align center	⌘+ E
Align left	⌘+ L
Display the **Modify Cell Style** dialog box	⌘+ SHIFT + L
Display the **Format Cells** dialog box	⌘+ 1
Apply the general number format	CONTROL + SHIFT + ~
Apply the currency format with two decimal places (negative numbers appear in red with parentheses)	CONTROL + SHIFT + $
Apply the percentage format with no decimal places	CONTROL + SHIFT + %
Apply the exponential number format with two decimal places	CONTROL + SHIFT + ^
Apply the date format with the day, month, and year	CONTROL + SHIFT + #
Apply the time format with the hour and minute, and indicate A.M. or P.M.	CONTROL + SHIFT + @

Apply the number format with two decimal places, thousands separator, and minus sign (-) for negative values	CONTROL + SHIFT + !
Apply the outline border around the selected cells	⌘+ OPTION + ZERO
Add an outline border to the right of the selection	⌘+ OPTION + RIGHT ARROW
Add an outline border to the left of the selection	⌘+ OPTION + LEFT ARROW
Add an outline border to the top of the selection	⌘+ OPTION + UP ARROW
Add an outline border to the bottom of the selection	⌘+ OPTION + DOWN ARROW
Remove outline borders	⌘+ OPTION + HYPHEN
Apply or remove bold formatting	⌘+ B
Apply or remove italic formatting	⌘+ I
Apply or remove underscoring	⌘+ U
Apply or remove strikethrough formatting	⌘+ SHIFT + X
Hide a column	⌘+) or CONTROL +)
Unhide a column	⌘+ SHIFT +) or CONTROL + SHIFT +)
Hide a row	⌘+ (or CONTROL + (

Unhide a row	⌘+ SHIFT + (or CONTROL + SHIFT + (
Edit the active cell	CONTROL + U
Cancel an entry in the cell or the formula bar	ESC
Edit the active cell and then clear it, or delete the preceding character in the active cell as you edit the cell contents	DELETE
Paste text into the active cell	⌘+ V
Complete a cell entry	RETURN
Give selected cells the current cell's entry	⌘+ RETURN or CONTROL + RETURN
Enter a formula as an array formula	⌘+ SHIFT + RETURN or CONTROL + SHIFT + RETURN
Display the Formula Builder after you type a valid function name in a formula	CONTROL + A

Work With a Selection

TASK	SHORTCUT
Copy	⌘+ C or CONTROL + V

Paste	⌘+ V or CONTROL + V
Cut	⌘+ X or CONTROL + X
Clear	DELETE
Delete the selection	CONTROL + HYPHEN
Undo the last action	⌘+ Z
Hide a column	⌘+) or CONTROL +)
Unhide a column	⌘+ SHIFT +) or CONTROL + SHIFT +)
Hide a row	⌘+ (or CONTROL + (
Unhide a row	⌘+ SHIFT + (or CONTROL + SHIFT + (
Move from top to bottom within the selection (down) *	RETURN
Move from bottom to top within the selection (up) *	SHIFT + RETURN
Move from left to right within the selection, or move down one cell if only one column is selected	TAB

Move from right to left within the selection, or move up one cell if only one column is selected	SHIFT + TAB
Move clockwise to the next corner of the selection	CONTROL + PERIOD
Group selected cells	⌘+ SHIFT + K
Ungroup selected cells	⌘+ SHIFT + J

* These shortcuts may move in another direction other than down or up. If you'd like to change the direction of these shortcuts, click the **Excel** menu, and then click **Preferences**. Click **Edit**. Then change the direction for **After pressing Return, move selection**.

Select Cells, Columns, or Rows.

Note: If a function key doesn't work as you expect it to, press the **FN** key in addition to the function key. If you don't want to press the FN key each time, you can change your system preferences: Go to **Apple > System Preferences > Keyboard**. Then select the check box for **Use all F1, F2, etc. as standard function keys**.

TASK	SHORTCUT
Extend the selection by one cell	SHIFT + arrow key
Extend the selection to the last nonblank cell	⌘+ SHIFT + arrow key

in the same column or row as the active cell	
Extend the selection to the beginning of the row	SHIFT + HOME
Extend the selection to the beginning of the sheet	CONTROL + SHIFT + HOME
Extend the selection to the last cell used on the sheet (lower-right corner)	CONTROL + SHIFT + END
Select the entire column	CONTROL + SPACEBAR
Select the entire row	SHIFT + SPACEBAR
Select the entire sheet	⌘ + A
Select only visible cells	⌘ + SHIFT + * (asterisk)
Select only the active cell when multiple cells are selected	SHIFT + DELETE
Extend the selection down one screen	SHIFT + PAGE DOWN
Extend the selection up one screen	SHIFT + PAGE UP
Alternate between hiding objects, displaying objects, and displaying placeholders for objects	CONTROL + 6
Turn on the capability to extend a selection by using the arrow keys	F8
Add another range of cells to the selection	SHIFT + F8

Select the current array, which is the array that the active cell belongs to	CONTROL + /
Select cells in a row that don't match the value in the active cell in that row. You must select the row starting with the active cell	CONTROL + \
Select only cells that are directly referred to by formulas in the selection	CONTROL + SHIFT + [
Select all cells that are directly or indirectly referred to by formulas in the selection	CONTROL + SHIFT + {
Select only cells with formulas that refer directly to the active cell	CONTROL +]
Select all cells with formulas that refer directly or indirectly to the active cell	CONTROL + SHIFT + }

Use Charts

Note: If a function key doesn't work as you expect it to, press the **FN** key in addition to the function key. If you don't want to press the FN key each time, you can change your system preferences: Go to **Apple > System Preferences > Keyboard**. Then select the check box for **Use all F1, F2, etc. as standard function keys**.

TASK	SHORTCUT

| Insert a new chart sheet. ** | F11 |
| Cycle through chart object selection | An arrow key |

** This shortcut conflicts with a default Mac OS key assignment. To use this shortcut, you must change your Mac keyboard settings. Go to **Apple** > **System Preferences** > **Keyboard** > **Shortcuts**. Click **Mission Control**, and then click to deselect the **Show Desktop** option.

Sort, Filter, and Use PivotTable Reports.

TASK	SHORTCUT
Open the **Sort** dialog box	⌘+ SHIFT + R
Add or remove a filter	⌘+ SHIFT + F or CONTROL + SHIFT + L
Display the Filter list or PivotTable page field pop-up menu for the selected cell	OPTION + DOWN ARROW

Outline Data

TASK	SHORTCUT
Display or hide outline symbols	CONTROL + 8
Hide selected rows	CONTROL + 9

Unhide selected rows	CONTROL + SHIFT + (
Hide selected columns	CONTROL + ZERO
Unhide selected columns	CONTROL + SHIFT +)

Work In Windows

Note: If a function key doesn't work as you expect it to, press the **FN** key in addition to the function key. If you don't want to press the FN key each time, you can change your system preferences: Go to **Apple** > **System Preferences** > **Keyboard**. Then select the check box for **Use all F1, F2, etc. as standard function keys**.

TASK	SHORTCUT
Expand or minimize the ribbon	⌘+ OPTION + R
Switch to full screen view	⌘+ CONTROL + F
Switch to the next application	⌘+ TAB
Switch to the previous application	⌘+ SHIFT + TAB
Close the active workbook window	⌘+ W
Copy the image of the screen and save it to a Screen Shot file on your desktop.	⌘+ SHIFT + 3
Minimize the active window	CONTROL + F9
Maximize or restore the active window	CONTROL + F10 or ⌘+ F10
Hide Excel.	⌘+ H

Work In Dialog Boxes

TASK	SHORTCUT
Move to the next text box	TAB
Move to the previous box, option, control, or command	SHIFT + TAB
Exit a dialog box or cancel an action	ESC
Perform the action assigned to the default command button (the button with the bold outline, often the **OK** button)	RETURN
Cancel the command and close	ESC

Use Function Key Shortcuts

Excel for Mac 2016 uses the function keys for common commands, including Copy and Paste. For quick access to these shortcuts, you can change your Apple system preferences so you don't have to press the Fn key every time you use a function key shortcut

Note: Changing system function key preferences affects how the function keys work for your Mac, not just Excel. After changing this setting, you can still perform the special features printed on a function key. Just press the Fn key. For example, to use the F12 key to change your volume, you would press Fn+F12.

If a function key doesn't work as you expect it to, press the **FN** key in addition to the function key. If you don't want to press the FN key each time, you can change your Apple system preferences:

Change function key preferences with the mouse

1. On the **Apple** menu, press **System Preferences**.
2. Select **Keyboard**.
3. On the **Keyboard** tab, select the check box for **Use all F1, F2, etc. keys as standard function keys**.

CHAPTER 7.

Bonus Section

Safari 9 (El Capitan): Safari Keyboard and Other Shortcuts.

Safari is an internet browser developed by Apple Inc. that goes with Mac computers. It is fast and more energy efficient than any other browser as far as browsing with Macintosh computers are concerned.

This is a list of keyboard shortcuts you can use, in addition to those that appear in Safari menus.

Webpages

TASK	SHORTCUT
Scroll up, down, left, or right	Press the arrow keys.
Scroll in larger increments	Press Option while you press an arrow key.
Scroll down a screen	Page Down Space bar
Scroll up a screen	Page Up Shift–Space bar

Scroll to the top-left or bottom-left corner of the page	Command–Up Arrow or Home Command–Down Arrow or End
Highlight the next item on a webpage	Tab highlights the next text field or pop-up menu. Tab also highlights buttons and other controls if "All controls" is selected in the Shortcuts pane of the Keyboard pane of System Preferences. Option-Tab highlights the same items as Tab plus all other clickable items. To swap the behavior of Tab and Option-Tab, turn on "Press Tab to highlight each item on a webpage" in the Advanced pane of Safari preferences.
Open a page in a new tab	Command-click a link Command-click a bookmark Command-Return after typing in the Smart Search field.
Open a page in a new tab, and bring the tab to the front	Shift-Command-click a link Shift-Command-click a bookmark

	Shift-Command-Return after typing in the Smart Search field.
Bring the next tab to the front	Control-Tab or Shift-Command-]
Bring the previous tab to the front	Control-Shift-Tab or Shift-Command -[
Select one of your first nine tabs	Command-1 to Command-9
Close all tabs except for one	Option-click the close button (X) on the tab you want to leave open
Open in tabs all the bookmarks in a folder in the Favorites bar	Command-click the folder in the Favorites bar
See a list of recent pages by name	Hold down the Back or Forward button until the list appears
See a list of recent pages by web address (URL)	Press Option and hold down the Back or Forward button until the list appears
Go to your homepage	Command-Home key
While typing in the Smart Search field, restore the current webpage address	Esc
Close Reader	Esc
Exit full-screen view	Esc

Download a linked file	Option-click a link to the file
Open a downloaded file	Double-click the file in the downloads list

Reading List

TASK	SHORTCUT
Add the current page	Shift-Command-D
Add a linked page	Shift-click a link to the page
Remove a page	Swipe left over the page summary using a trackpad or mouse that supports gestures, then click Remove. Or, swipe all the way to the left until the page summary disappears.

Bookmarks

TASK	SHORTCUT
Add a bookmark to the Favorites bar	Click the Smart Search field to show the page's full address and its icon, then drag the icon to the Favorites bar
Move a bookmark on the Favorites bar	Drag the bookmark left or right

Remove a bookmark from the Favorites bar	Drag the bookmark off the top of the bar

Bookmarks Sidebar and Bookmarks View

TASK	SHORTCUT
Select bookmarks and folders in the sidebar	Command-click each bookmark and folder Shift-click to extend the selection
Select the next bookmark or folder	Up Arrow or Down Arrow
Open the selected bookmark	Space bar
Open the selected folder	Space bar or Right Arrow
Close the selected folder	Space bar or Left Arrow
Open the selected folder and its subfolders in the sidebar	Option–Right Arrow
Close the selected folder and its subfolders in the sidebar	Option–Left Arrow
Change the name or address of a bookmark	Select the bookmark, then press Return
Cancel editing a bookmark name in the sidebar	Esc

Finish editing a bookmark name	Return
Create a folder containing the selected bookmarks and folders in bookmarks view	Option-click the New Folder button at the bottom of the window
Delete a bookmark	Select the bookmark, then press Delete

Customer's Page.

This page is for customers who enjoyed Microsoft Excel 2016 Keyboard Shortcuts For Macintosh.

Dearly beloved customer, please leave a review behind if you enjoyed this book or found it helpful. It will be highly appreciated, thank you.

Download Our Free EBooks Today.

In order to appreciate our customers, we have made some of our titles available at 0.00. Totally free. Feel free to get a copy of the free titles.

(A) For Keyboard Shortcuts In Windows

Go to Amazon: <u>Windows 7 Keyboard shortcuts</u>

Go to Other Stores: <u>Windows 7 Keyboard Shortcuts</u>

(B) For Keyboard Shortcuts In Office 2016

Go to Amazon: <u>Word 2016 Keyboard Shortcuts For windows</u>

Go to Other Stores: <u>Word 2016 Keyboard Shortcuts For Windows</u>

Note: Feel free to download them from your favorite store today. Thank you!

Other Books By This Publisher.

S/N	Title	Series
Series A: Limits Breaking Quotes.		
1	Discover Your Key Christian Quotes	Limits Breaking Quotes
Series B: Shortcut Matters.		
1	Windows 7 Shortcuts	Shortcut Matters
2	Windows 7 Shortcuts & Tips	Shortcut Matters
3	Windows 8.1 Shortcuts	Shortcut Matters
4	Windows 10 Shortcut Keys	Shortcut Matters
5	Microsoft Office 2007 Keyboard Shortcuts For Windows.	Shortcut Matters
6	Microsoft Office 2010 Shortcuts For Windows.	Shortcut Matters
7	Microsoft Office 2013 Shortcuts For Windows.	Shortcut Matters
8	Microsoft Office 2016 Shortcuts For Windows.	Shortcut Matters
Series C: Teach Yourself.		
1	Teach Yourself Computer Fundamentals	Teach Yourself
Series D: For Painless Publishing		
1	Self-Publish it with CreateSpace.	For Painless Publishing
2	Where is my money? Now solved for Kindle and CreateSpace	For Painless Publishing
3	Describe it on Amazon	For Painless Publishing
4	How To Market That Book.	For Painless Publishing